T0290389

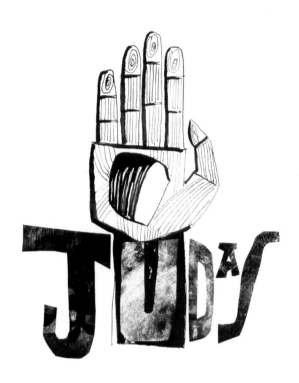

for Kevin Mills

Judas

Damian Walford Davies

SEREN

Seren is the book imprint of
Poetry Wales Press Ltd.
57 Nolton Street, Bridgend, Wales, CF31 3AE
www.serenbooks.com
facebook.com/SerenBooks
twitter@SerenBooks

The right of Damian Walford Davies to be identified as
the author of this work has been asserted in accordance
with the Copyright, Designs and Patents Act, 1988.

© Damian Walford Davies 2015

ISBN: 978-1-78172-222-0
e-book: 978-1-78172-223-7
Kindle: 978-1-78172-225-1

A CIP record for this title is available from the British Library.

The publisher acknowledges the financial assistance of the Welsh Books Council.

Book Cover Design and interior decorations by Clive Hicks-Jenkins.

Author website: http://dwalforddavies.wix.com/damianwalforddavies

Contents

You will be cursed by the other generations – and you will come to rule over them…. Lift up your eyes and look at the cloud and the light within it and the stars surrounding it. The star that leads the way is your star.
   – Jesus to Judas, *The Gospel of Judas* (mid-2nd century CE)

…in saying that the viscera of Iscariot, or his middle, had burst and gushed out, the original reporter meant simply that his heart had broke.
   – Thomas De Quincey, 'Judas Iscariot' (1857)

I am surely his familiar friend.
   – Judas of Jesus, Aaron Dwight Baldwin, *The Gospel of Judas Iscariot* (1902)

…men shall bless me because I had boldness and was not afraid, but went right onward and did this thing.
   – George A. Page, *The Diary of Judas Iscariot* (1912)

Another ordinary appalled man.
   – Brendan Kennelly, *The Book of Judas* (1991)

Valley

I know my script-
ure: this tomb-pocked wadi's
where we're one day

meant to jostle – bones
and tatty sinews,
Jew and Gentile –

at the Judgement.
Those just-trussed,
aloe-sweetened bodies

stiffening in the rock
will steal a march
on all of us. I'm just

a shadow lengthening
in this thistled river-bed,
expecting nothing

but the sun to dip behind
the bluff cubes of a city
no differently from yesterday.

Denominations

You'll paint me gross –
gripping my shins,
retching silver coins.

Let me put you straight.
All I've got's loose change
for late-night kofta stands

outside the Lions' Gate,
where tote-bag tourists
sip tart tamarind

from paper cups.
On Friday night I saw the city
wane and wax to pixels

on the screens of untold
mobile phones. From unbuilt
minarets, muezzins hoist

the pale Passover moon
above the gospel
of the Separation Wall.

Fauna

The night's astray
with dogs. A starving bitch,
half jackal, works the neon

tombslabs on the slope.
All the world's downwind.
Have you ever scoped

a kill? Look – the body
halts, then bows,
as if conceding to a partner

in a dance. A tremor thrills
the pelt; now the pounce
into the blue scream

of the scrub. That snatch
will see her for another week.
Tomorrow's Monday.

Wake me at first light; we'll gauge
the quarry from the gross
conundrum of the flesh.

Gnosis

You can't know red
until you see the shock
of lambsblood on the gold

stones of the temple court;
or phony, till you clock
two women kissing

air above each other's
shoulders in the lobby
of the Sheraton;

fear, until you watch
a teenage soldier
realise he's big enough

to drive a nail through wrists
and heels; or joy,
until you see the downtown

mural of that uzi-toting
trooper frisked by girls;
or lies, until you've heard me out.

Play

Father Abraham
knelt on this rock, knee
in the small of his stunned

son's back, crabbed fist
fast in a shock of curls,
knifeblade bright

with brinkmanship.
Off Haifa Street
when I was nine,

smashed squaddies
posed my father
with a dagger at my throat.

I faked terror like a pro.
Knowing how it ends –
deus ex machina angel,

magicked ram –
I lay there jaded, waiting
for them all to bottle out.

Siloam Pool

With each new body
sliding in, the water
overflows the topmost

step, then finds its level.
Small tarns of overspill
evaporate to bedrock

on the sides. I'm trying
to forget my flesh,
the only sound

the lapping of the basin's
fickle tide.
Below the spring,

dishes point to Mecca.
Let me wash; I'll come clean
and meet you in a bar

in Ben Yehuda Street.
We'll talk
about the elephant in the room.

Bread

These are the chic boutiques
that even monogram
the wrapping crêpe –

cerements for when
the next blast
blows the street

to kingdom come. I know
this neighbourhood
as deadpan plain

beyond the city walls,
a place to shake the dust
from tattered shoes

just past the Jaffa sign.
I'll choose the wine; you
pour – my hand's not steady

yet. I'll take and bless
and break the pretzels,
since they're bread.

Is-Kariot

Years of rope will chafe
a channel in the limestone
lips of wells

and buff the grooves
to marble.
This is a parable of how

the slights of fatmen,
landlords, petty managers,
abrades a bitter runnel

in the brain that's vexed
to smoothness.
All day my mother's hands

are flayed in fields
we owned near Kariot,
where birds

bust up in clouds
with every *phut-phut*
of the firing range.

Annunciation 1

It was an August Shabbat.
I was twenty-six.
Like broken legs,

our flails hung
in the threshing room,
air wheaten, muzzy.

I was watching two grey
butcherbirds impale
a brace of bees

on thistle thorns.
(No parable.)
Leaching from the idle

olive press,
a shadow kinked
across the grass. *I know*

you love enough,
it said. *I'll teach you*
how to hit and run.

Contract

A good kill's clean,
without collateral,
target down

before he even feels
the knife. I learned to be
anonymous, another body

in a surging crowd,
shrill owlcry
from beyond the date palms,

silence when the nervy soldiers
halt. At spendthrift galas
others gawked

at golden surplices,
sharp suits; I was drilled
to see the hidden artery.

One thrust, if deep,
brings out a dazzling
arc of blood.

In Vino

No depth, no heft,
no body: this bottle's
from the Hebron outposts

where the vinestock's
still too young.
What's spilt dries fast

in darkening crescents
on our coasters,
stamped with David's star.

You think I'm stalling,
buying time.
We'll go the long way

home, past Yad Vashem;
I'll wait outside;
go see the gallery

of ghetto faces
in the boxcar, cheek-to-cheek
like Tishbi grapes.

Suburbia

I know I said I'd wait;
two teenage conscripts
ordered me to move along,

penned me
in the lattice-lanes
off Jabotinsky, radios

sputtering in tongues.
I lost them in Rihavia,
where the Eged buses

keep their engines ticking
over in the plaza's
choked hypotenuse.

I'm aiming for the tumbled
neighbourhood you'll raze
to build the ballpark walkway

to the tufted Wall, where
rocking men and rookies
poke prayers in nooks and cracks.

Sanctuary

Three streets away
the afternoon patrol
beats out the early days

of Anno Domini.
That's the name
let loose. Time to call

some favours in.
I know a city-centre
safe house where they

trim wicks low
in last year's olive oil,
light up

only when the lookout
tips the wink.
My calling card's

the henna skull tattoo
I sat for
in a previous life.

Annunciation 2

Pinch out all the lamps;
I want to raise him
in the dark.

It was the morning after
the Ramla job.
I'd bodged it – cockeyed

lunge, my rash stab
out of true. I drowned it all

in moonshine, woke
in backstreet Mea Shearim
to find the city

liverish. Damascene? –
don't make me...
Fugged, I fathomed out

a torso blotting out
the sun. *Stand and
sober up*, he said. *You stink.*

Dog

I lashed out, lost
him in the steam
from laundromats

where Zonnenfelt
meets Reichman
in a crux. You'll say:

how very noir.
That day he dogged me
chronic: beggars

kvetching for my coins
held out *his* hands;
he was the shyster

hawking joblots,
the kid who sold me
borscht. Listing queazy

in the barber's chair,
I saw him flash across
the mirror's face.

Rolling Stone

Winding down to Nablus,
halfway anywhere,
Highway 60 waving

into water up ahead,
I caught him
standing scarecrow

in a cornfield, playing
to a folky freetrade crowd.
It looked like crazed

charades – *song;
one Word; two syllables;
sounds like...*

Behind him, blinds
came down in Bet El's
ritzy newbuilds.

His thumbs-up seemed
to set off car alarms.
Play it fucking loud.

Scouting

Two miles on
past Jacob's Well,
I fell among kibbutzniks

camped out
in an orange grove.
They had me stoned

by midnight, staring
at the moonlit
mirrorballs of fruit.

Then him again,
crouching at the centre
of our circle, madly

fretting wood for one
immaculate ember.
At last the tinder took.

Through swirls of citrus
smoke, I watched him
cradle bleeding palms.

Georgic

Look: around the shutters,
stains of light.
The lamps lacklustre.

To put it differently:
time to bail.
Where was I?

Walking north, that's right;
shadowed. I holed up
in a homestead,

took a job as gofer,
slipshod shepherd,
handyman.

From the off
the farm dogs skirred
and slunk from me.

I had my host's wife
weekly in the sharp,
black umbra of the barn.

Prompt

Blessed are the meek,
he barked,
for they shall —

and he choked.
His silence fell
on stony ground, the sea

of chapped, flint faces
churning into scowls.
His right hand

paddled air, groping
for a windfall epigram.
Nothing came.

For they shall
WHAT? one called.
Inherit the earth?

I offered, leaning in.
But you'll have to
tell them when.

Tilapia Zillii

From the terraces,
tares' fifth columns
mimicking the wheat,

you could see
the morning launches
harrowing the lake,

black nets broadcast
like sprays of seed.
Voices travelled, bickering

on the easterlies:
a rogue boat drifted
from its sanctioned

pitch – a rival cast
too close – a patched-up
trammel ripped. And all

for petty hauls
of blotched and spiny
bastard-ugly fish.

Peripheral

I learned a louche routine,
filled out, found
thirteen shades of autumn

in a lengthening beard.
I bluffed the fishers'
patter, parroted

their burr and drawl.
In baskets on the jetties
silver slabs of muscle

twitched and flexed.
They weighed the earth.
He happened always

at the edges of the eye,
coming into focus
like rocks unrippling

through a dying wake.
Each handshake left you
with scale-spangled skin.

Query

*Who do you say
I am?* he posed,
apropos of nothing,

his gutting knife
poised at the rude
gash of a gill.

Out rolled
the same old
smooth replies.

I was tugging free
the lewd slug of a liver.
Who do you *say*

you *are?* I asked.
He resumed the knife's
intimate intifada,

its flashing
hack and slash
a retort of sorts.

Magdalen

She was a piece
of work: deft
where they were brute,

harpstring-taut
against their oafishness.
She pulsed on frequencies

beyond their range.
He tuned himself
to her, but feared

his body's
rough reply.
I'd prickle

hours before she came
in range – kept
my distance,

knowing she'd be tart,
a bitter medlar
on the tongue.

Forecast

Give me a trade of clothes
against the light's
striptease – something

cowled, no logo –
to get me back inside
the Zion Gate,

where street kids sail
frail navies in a lead-lined
cistern, playing commodores.

Breezes send the cork tops
veering into troughs.
I saw it on the lake:

from nowhere, killing
cloudbursts, whiplash
skeins of spray.

Here we are. Let's kneel,
consider how that insect's
footfalls make the surface bend.

Kosher

A crowd-surge
turned them into
bodyguards, linked arms

forming cordons round him
as he hollered soundbites,
punchlines to his latest

prayers. Hustled to a waiting
boat, he lay
dead-eyed in bilge

among the weights
and blackening hooks.
They put to sea

theatrically. I watched
until the skyline blanched them
out. I wasn't there to see him

rid the hobo of his rattled
Legion, missed the panic
of the screwball swine.

Like

Branched sage
was blooming yellow
on the wayside

and here's me
telling him: spare me
the eternal similes:

like seed, like nets,
like this man,
like another; like

a child. This is worse
than dark. Tell it like
it is. He stopped;

that maddening smile
again. He said:
the kingdom is...

and tapped a finger
on my chest. The scent
of sage was like a song.

Game

Watch your step:
these stones, one day,
will wear to glass.

He was kneeling here,
scruffing off the dust,
exposing hopscotch

squares. They lugged
the tangled, bucking
woman to his side,

nipples hard with fear,
and ranged themselves
round little magazines

of rock. He flinched,
but kept on scouring
with his stick. At last

he raised a pebble,
aimed, and threw.
Encouraged them to skip.

Armageddon

Of course
there were dreams:
I'd conjure him

as house-to-house guerrilla,
captaining the push
down Paratroopers Road.

I'd have him breach
the vanguard
on a madcap horse,

turn four faces
like Ezekiel's cherubim.
Or he'd enter

at the Golden Gate,
the sky imperial:
standing water

jetting up as geysers,
woken bodies
thrashing through the soil.

Puppet

Their timing was
impeccable: he'd botched
a spiel on love – failed

to find the figure
that would salvage it –
and suddenly the air

was thick with braids
of straw; the sun
blazed in and was

eclipsed; we watched
a body drop
in stuttered phases

to his feet, rope skeins
thrashing down
in helixes. He raised it

by the armpits,
made it dance a jig
among the pricking stalks.

Twitching

See, the swifts are back.
Black devils
locked in dog-fights,

shadows screamed
on stone. They say
they never leave us,

that they sleep in pools.
Have you noticed
how the sunbirds

start up only when
the echo of the call to prayer
gives up the ghost?

Or how a crow
drops stones in cisterns
till the water

rises to its flickering
black tongue? Forgive
these trifling nature notes.

Alarm

I'd wake to find him
hunkered, panicked
by the bandaged,

pawing hands,
his body given
to their hankering.

Some chased
the dark shroud
of his shadow,

as if that
were also flesh.
I trained myself to rise

before the ragged knots
came shambling
down the hill;

I'd fret him
from his sleep
with pleading palms.

Leash

I asked him
where he stood on ghosts.
(I'd seen my father

in the fields –
grey-green, electric,
like his kilt of corn.)

He cited deadman
Samuel – subpoenaed,
peeved and jawing,

at a séance;
did I not believe
in that? I said again

I'd seen my old man
swaying in a shock
of stalks. He cried:

*I see a spirit
after you; will I let it
slip the leash?*

Confection

On Khan al-Zeit
they're scooping out the spices
into coloured dunes

that loosen into landslides
as the day wears down.
Sweet disputing sour

in the throat,
we'd dodge the crazy
barrow-boys on Sundays

with their shrill
Al-o! Al-o!
He'd run his fingers

through the jangling
tourist tat, dally
near the candy stalls,

judge the sugared melons –
lime-laced jellies –
worlds of rainbow jubes.

Ferae Naturae

City of cats! Eyeless,
crooked, scarred – all born
survivors. I'll take

the hint: fight,
fake buckled limbs,
scratch skin red-raw,

live in grungy colonies
in courtyards rank
with refuse sluiced out

from the souqs, one eye
peeled for tomcats
sniffing round

my pissing ground.
I could hump a living
from these streets,

yowl to other outposts
from the floodlit
ashlar of the Wall.

Lido

Bethesda of the agitated
pool... I'm waxing lyrical.
He helped me haul

my father here
one faddy spring. We waited

for the flighty angel's
troubling of the tarn.
Cradling him, we saw

the surface pucker,
rushed to hup him in.
His waistcloth

bloated to the surface
like a bloom. We beached
the same old withered

legs — twisted gorgeously
(he offered)
like the blasé angel's hair.

Draft

Easy, now. Marking time
in Hurva Square,
sweating out the juice

from last night's jag
in Tel Aviv,
teen conscripts lounge

against the limes,
buzzcut scalps
red-raw as nutmeg,

dance tunes
banging in the skull,
eyes trailing

high-pitched hemlines,
pigeons' patterns
like Haredi curls,

fingers growing
callous
on the safety catch.

Rhetoric

Little Babylon
he called those tumbling
hillside gardens

of the Temple priests –
oases struck
from po-faced rock

as if by Aaron's rod.
He'd riff
on Neb'chadnezzar's terrors

in the marble rooms,
serpents
in the ritzy colonnades.

Words, words, words!
I'd tell him
when he came off stage;

just words, words,
words! Just
words, just words!

J. Wept

What happened
in the gravethroat
quite depends. I saw him

flail and punch the rockface,
but the dark was plush
and I was hardly

ringside. He bayed
his grief, trading echoes
with the walls –

it seemed the deadman
was awake and howling
too. The best seats say

he bent to parse the lattice
of the linen face, sucking up
the smack of myrrh,

mulled now with perished
flesh. And then – we all agree –
the crooning of a lullaby.

Barfly

I need a shot of arac
to char the gut.
Barman: go bleed

the optic dry;
I'll watch it charge itself
behind your back.

My neighbour grips
his spotlit bourbon
at a raking slant,

ice cubes fading
to their cloudy cores.
His partner excavates

a cocktail with a gaudy
straw, dab hand
busy in the dark

beneath the brushed-steel
rail. The spirit quavers
in his golden glass.

Stellar

I've made it to mid-week –
neither beaten up
nor born again.

The city cools:
crowds thin;
prices are adjusted

in the hostelries.
Dusk gazumps
the suburbs,

pricking out the stars –
patterns broken
only by an airplane's

lightpulse,
heading out transjordan
to the dark,

faith pinned
on a runway
east of Eden.

Admission

That line of silver, arcing
through the olive groves –
that's last week's shortcut

into town. He ditched
his cockeyed ride
before we reached the gate;

left it roadside, braying
blasphemies. There was
a token crowd. A soldier watched;

the camber of his eyebrow
saying: *Back home we do*
triumphal entries, too;

larger, though,
with elephants. Palm fronds
slashed our shins to shreds.

We shambled back,
pale pustule-olives
harder than their stony hearts.

Anointing

It would have fetched
a ransom, but he let her
smash the alabaster jar

and daub him
till his hair was sleek,
the whole house rash

with musk. All I smelt
was ready cash dispersing
from his oil-slick flesh.

When she bent
to smear his feet, I lost it –
slapped the potsherd

from her hand.
He shot up, shimmering.
Foreheads locked, we synched

our breath. It was kissing,
almost. I think
I was the first to break.

Tellers

Meet you at two, he said,
at the Temple's business end.
I got there early, judged

the heifers' haunches,
cooed through wicker bars
at rubbernecking doves,

their crimson club-feet
twisted into balls. He tore in
feral, cracking bullwhips –

lashed air cracking
at their tips. I loved it:
tables turned, stone

thrashed, wings broken
in the tumbling cages,
silver tetradrachmas

showering the quad –
the foreign eagle
shocking on the thunderbolt.

Garden

He was leaning
on the muscled torso
of a tree, eyes soldered

to the moonlit
tesserae of tombs
two hundred yards away.

The plot was offering up
its scents: I remember
acid spearmint,

sour rue, and basil,
candysweet.
I whispered: *Run!* –

the ghost itch of the dagger
at my side.
Moths flickered

near his face, lured
by the bitter nectar
of his sweat.

Summary

I spent the way wee hours
watching torchflame
sicken into day.

At six he stumbled,
bound and blinking,
into no-man's-light.

At eight, two blocks away,
the gates rolled back
to frame his flayed flesh

swaying in the sand.
Queer: when they lashed him
to the crossbeam, he balanced

like a pair of scales.
I was close enough to see
the matted helix

of a strand of hair.
Around his streaming shins
two cats curled, lovingly.

Corpus

What can I say? I wasn't there:
neither ready to relieve him
of the transom's heft

at Via Dolorosa, Station number five;
nor standing with his mother
on the quarry's scree

to watch his wrists
spiked expertly
between electric nerve

and bone, and hear him
gurgle, drowning in the liquor
of his lungs. I could have tracked

the trail of blood
from here to where the last gob
hit the ground. The morning

had an air of perfect
commonplace. I howled,
so silently I know he heard.

Fizz

Early Sunday I went up there,
bribed the guards
with twists of sherbert,

left them laughing
at the technicolour
of each other's tongues.

I found the mill-stone
airtight on the tomb.
From a distance,

one eye closed,
I placed two fingers
round the stopgap rock

and played at rolling it away –
as now I break
this soda's seal,

turn the bevelled cap
to hear the spirit hissing
from the black solution's heart.

Compline

A desert wind burns in
through Hinnom,
finds me even in the kennel

of this cleft. I've woken hourly,
choking on the claggy sand.
So help me wrap

this ravelled cloak
around me, tight and total
like a shroud.

Last night, you say,
strange tongues of flame
descended on the rump

in upstairs rooms. I'll wake
a spook; take my pick
of compass points;

brace myself to be
the dark conductor
of your lightning strikes.

Acknowledgements

Thanks are due to the editors of the following magazines in which some of the poems in this book first appeared: *Poetry Wales; Planet: The Welsh Internationalist; New Welsh Review.*

I am also indebted to the University Research Fund of Aberystwyth University, which allowed me, in April 2012, to get to know the streets and souqs of Judas's Jerusalem.

About the Author

Damian Walford Davies was born in Aberystwyth in 1971. He is Professor of English and Head of the School of English, Communication & Philosophy at Cardiff University. He has published two previous collections with Seren: *Suit of Lights* (2009) and *Witch* (2012). Two recent volumes – *Poets' Graves* (2014) and *Ancestral Houses: The Lost Mansions of Wales* (2012) – offer creative engagements with place and the visual image (two fields in which his poetry is powerfully invested). A literary critic, theorist and editor as well as a poet, he has published widely on Romantic-period literature and culture and on the two literatures of Wales, his latest study being *Cartographies of Culture: New Geographies of Welsh Writing in English*. He is a regular contributor to arts programmes on television and radio. He is Chair of Literature Wales and is a regular performer at the Hay Festival.

Also by Damian Walford Davies

'*crackles with intelligence and inventiveness... a performer with great panache and stylistic verve.*'
   – Nicholas Murray, *Planet: The Welsh Internationalist*

'*wittily judged. The diction pulses with the power of different registers and the accompanying emotional gear-changes are psychologically satisfying. Above all, there is a musical rightness...*'
   – John Redmond, *New Welsh Review*

'*Astonishing, knock-you-backwards work... startlingly different.*'
   – Jane Holland, *www.handstar.co.uk*

'*tender, shocking, playful, sharp-eyed – a suitably sparkling performance.*'
   – Caroline Clark, *Gwales*

'*His lines startle with freshness and animation... hung like notes of music... refined, but never squeamish... encompass[ing] modern mess and myth... not decorative, but keenly political... outstanding...*'
   – Alison Brackenbury

'*Verse with content that stretches the ways to write...we need more like this.*'
   – Peter Finch, *peterfinchpoet.blogspot.com*

'as colourfully dramatic in its way as The Crucible... an unsettling
and original masterpiece.'
– Bernard O'Donoghue

'masterly.'
– Alice Entwistle, *Poetry Wales*

'Richly detailed and engrossing... vividly imaginative and intelligent.'
– Jane Yeh, *New Welsh Review*

'brooding... fascinating and deeply unsettling... an irresistible narrative
drive.' – Laura Wainwright, *www.walesartsreview.org*

*A remarkable work, at once poetic sequence, play and novel... the
poems crackle with emotion and brilliantly evoke time and place...
like Arthur Miller and Carol Churchill, this artist continues to
understand, depict and warn.'
– Caroline Clark, *Gwales*